JOAN BAEZ SUITE
for solo guitar

by JOHN DUARTE
written for SHARON ISBIN

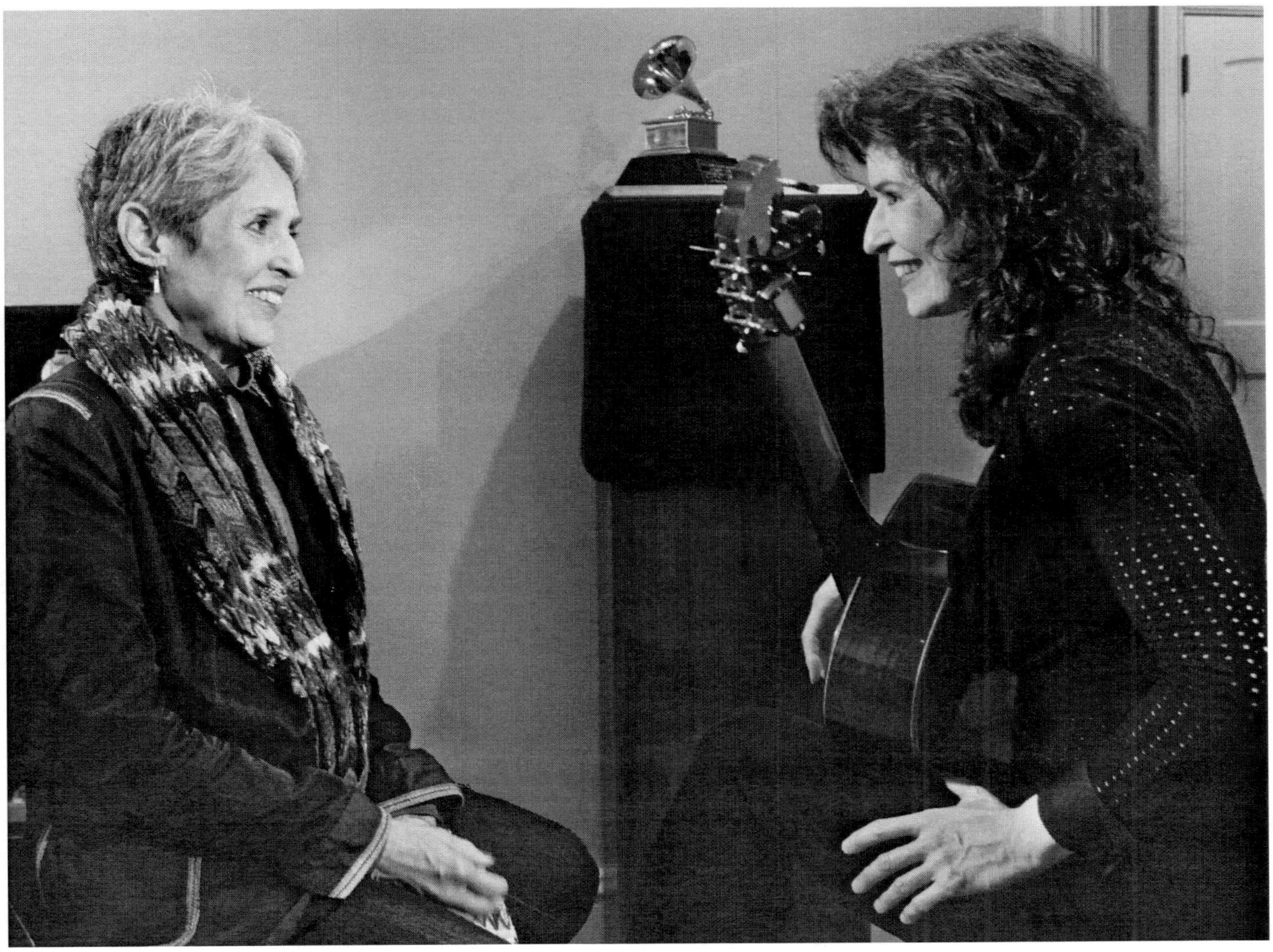

Joan Baez and Sharon Isbin in New York City with GRAMMY Award for Journey to the New World.

Exclusive Sales Agent: Mel Bay Publications, Inc.

WWW.MELBAY.COM

Program Notes

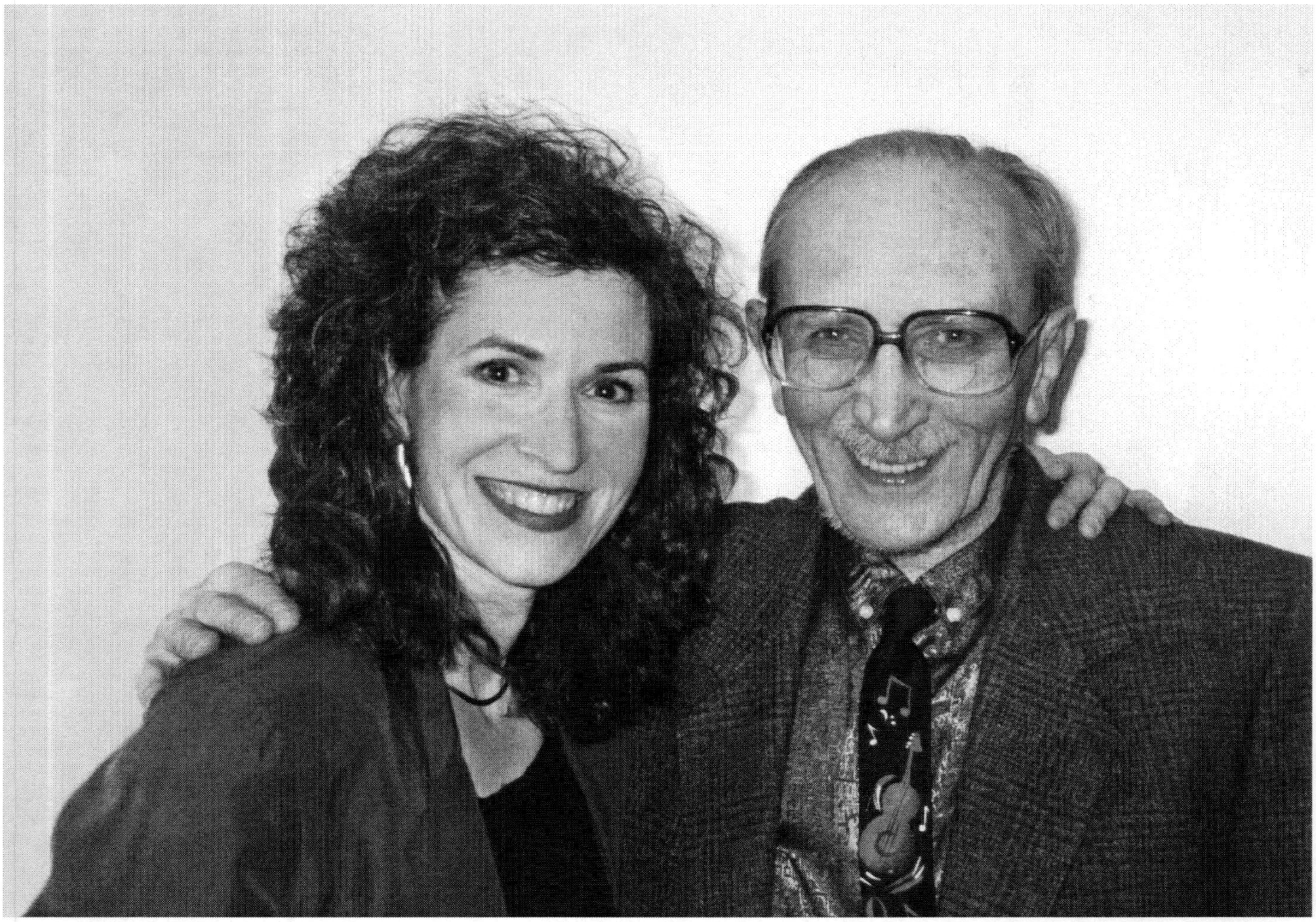

John Duarte and Sharon Isbin in New York City, February 1999 - Photo courtesy of and © Sharon Isbin.

World Première Recording:

Sharon Isbin: Journey to the New World (with guests Joan Baez and Mark O'Connor)
Sony Classical 88697-454562-0
Winner 2010 GRAMMY Award for Best Instrumental Soloist Performance

World Première:

Sharon Isbin, October 3, 2003, Herbst Hall, San Francisco Performances, San Francisco, CA, USA

Joan Baez and Sharon Isbin discuss their collaboration with music excerpts in the documentary **Sharon Isbin: Troubadour,** presented by American Public Television on PBS and winner of the 2015 ASCAP Television Broadcast Award. The film is available on DVD (4580) and Blu-ray (BD8202) from Video Artists International.

"Sharon's exquisite playing allowed me to revisit and fall in love with these songs all over again." – *Joan Baez*

Contents

Note: John Duarte's arrangement of the song *Where Have All the Flowers Gone?* has been omitted due to print license terms. This arrangement can be found at www.sheetmusicplus.com

Joan Baez Suite (2002) – John Duarte

Born 2 October 1919; died 23 December 2004

WRITTEN FOR SHARON ISBIN IN 2002, the *Joan Baez Suite* was commissioned with funds kindly provided by Rose Augustine and the Augustine Foundation. It is dedicated to the memory of Jody Nordlof.

I am old enough to have known and admired Joan Baez's work from the earliest years of her career. In writing this Suite it would, however, have been misguided to attempt to arrange the selected songs in the same style and format as hers. My settings represent my own reactions to the spirit and texts of the songs.

The opening *Fantasia* brings together three songs: *Once I Had a Sweetheart* is a song of frustrated love, with five-bar phrases. *Rambler Gambler* is an American adaptation of an English lyric song, sung by a man who doesn't care what others think about his attitude to life. He too experienced a love affair that ended unhappily. The English ballad *Barbara Allen* records the death of a young man whose love for its eponym was not returned; filled with remorse, she dies on the next day.

The House of the Rising Sun is the lament of a girl (in its original form she was a miner's daughter) who served in a brothel of that name. The lyrics were 'soft-pedalled' in the version made popular in the 1960s. I have based my version of the tune on that of the American blues singer, the late Josh White, whom I knew.

Frustrated love rears its head again in *The Lily of the West,* the song of a man who stabbed to death his rival for the affection of Flora 'the lily of the west' and remained cheerfully unrepentant to the end.

The Unquiet Grave is an English folk song of love, death and grief, sung by a girl whose loved one has died. In its final appearance in this arrangement I have counterpointed it with the melody of Dido's lament, from Henry Purcell's *Dido and Aeneas*. Dido, deserted by her lover Aeneas, sings "When I am laid in earth, remember me".

Silkie refers to the legendary 'sealfolk' (silkies) said to exist in the waters around the Orkney Islands (off the coast of Scotland). They were believed to be able to shed their skins and pass as human beings in order to find human partners! The tune is by Dr James Waters, a one-time professor at Columbia University. I have chosen to present it in the form of a simple set of Theme and Variations.

The *Finale*, like the opening *Fantasia*, introduces more than one tune: *Rake and Rambling Boy* is an English broadside ballad, recounted by the perpetrator of numerous crimes, some of them robbery from members of the aristocracy – for which he was finally hung on the gallows. With *Wildwood Flower* we are back to the lamentations of a girl (the eponymous 'flower') on the departure of her lover. The ballad has long been well known in the southern mountains, but its origin remains unknown. *The Trees They Do Grow High* is an English ballad about a boy married off to a young woman who waits impatiently for him to grow into adulthood (thus the analogy in the ever-rising accompaniment). At fifteen he becomes a father, but the joy is short-lived as he meets his death in battle within the year.

Foreword

John Duarte's position among the twentieth century traditions of the classical guitar is well assured for posterity. He was renowned for many activities including writer, lecturer, and teacher, as well as being one of the most prolific published composers for the instrument.

From the late 1930s onwards he wrote in various periodicals in characteristically acerbic manner highlighting the aesthetic deficiencies of the epoch in terms of plucked instruments. Over the years he formulated a new approach to critical appraisal of the role of the guitar in contemporary music, hoping and expecting standards to rise to the level of other more established instruments such as the piano or violin.

In the late 1940s and 1950s, with the arrival of Julian Bream and John Williams in the vanguard of a classical guitar revolution, John Duarte's former concepts found fulfilment. Now it was no longer Andrés Segovia who carried the banner of the guitar forward – the great Maestro had at last found his legacy in the concert hall fully realised. Over the years to come many fine and virtuosic musicians would become internationally respected guitar recitalists.

John Duarte's work over the next half century deepened in breadth and intensity. There was a great demand not only for critical competence in the writing of reviews and articles, but also ultimately a need for skilled teaching in many educational contexts, schools, colleges, summer festivals, and university campuses. John Duarte broadened his approach by writing for musical magazines such as *Records & Recording* and *Gramophone*. But at the same time he wrote a tremendous amount of pedagogic material, including articles in guitar periodicals, technique books, and compositions intended for apprentice guitarists of all ages.

But at heart John Duarte was a natural composer whose lively intelligence and extraordinary musical sensitivity gave rise to an immense output of creative energy. Music poured incessantly from his pen - solos, duets, quartets, ensemble music, sonatinas, variations, suites, concertos, songs, studies, impressionistic pieces, arrangements, etc. It was, and remains, a cornucopia of excellence, much of which has still to be evaluated and accorded its true worthy acknowledgement by contemporary performers. His music effortlessly encompasses many styles, many moods, and is invariably rewarding and enriching both to perform and to listen to.

It is thus with great pleasure, and a sense of privilege, that I am honoured to write this introduction for a new Duarte publication, the *Joan Baez Suite,* edited by that great guitarist Sharon Isbin (for whom the composer in 1996 wrote the suite Appalachian Dreams, the centrepiece of her album, *Dreams of a World,* for which she received a 2001 GRAMMY Award for Best Instrumental Soloist Performance).

The *Joan Baez Suite,* rooted in beautiful songs and arranged in the composer's inimitable style, provides a timely reminder of how much the classical guitar world of today is indebted to the life-long labours of John Duarte.

John Duarte

JOHN DUARTE was born on 2 October 1919 in Sheffield, England. He was 100% British despite his name having Portuguese overtones. His father was Scottish and his mother, who was born in Philadelphia, USA, was English!

He was educated at Manchester Central High School (1931-35) and Manchester University Faculty of Technology (1936-40). He worked as a professional chemist until 1969, then abandoned chemistry in favour of full-time music. His only formal musical education was lessons with Terence Usher (1934-36) in jazz-guitar playing; the rest was by self-instruction. His many friendships with great artists included one of 39 years with Andrés Segovia and an enforcedly shorter one with Ida Presti, who died at the age of 42.

He was the composer of nearly 150 works for the guitar and lute (many commissioned with funds provided by the Arts Council of Great Britain and other sources, official and private, both domestic and overseas). Many have been published and nearly half have been commercially recorded. He was also the author of very many arrangements (several also recorded) and didactic works.

As the writer of countless articles he was a regular contributor to *Soundboard,* interviewer and reviewer of books, music, concerts and recordings of many kinds in *Gramophone, Music Teacher* and *Classical Guitar,* and author of numerous concert-programme notes and about 250 liner notes for records and CDs of various kinds, including those for the complete reissue of Julian Bream's recordings for RCA (28 compact discs). He received a *GRAMMY Award* for his annotation to the reissue of Segovia's recordings of 1927-39 and his *Appalachian Dreams op.121* formed the centrepiece of the 2001 *GRAMMY Award*-winning album *Dreams of a World* by Sharon Isbin. He contributed regularly to *Music in Education, Guitar Review, Guitar International, Music & Musicians, Records and Recording,* and *Performance* and was a contributor to the revised edition of *The New Grove Dictionary of Music and Musicians.*

As a teacher he prepared many international students for successful careers, and he was Director of the Cannington International Guitar Summer School and Festival (1974-93), Course Director of the Bath International Guitar Festival (1994-95) and the Oatridge International Guitar Summer School and Festival (near Edinburgh, Scotland). He worked as a teacher, lecturer and adjudicator in 29 countries outside the United Kingdom.

At the Convention of the Guitar Foundation of America in October 1999 he received an Award for Lifetime Achievement.

Other Mel Bay publications by John Duarte

Three Compositions for Two Guitars –
Varieties of Scotch op.123 (1996); *Shades of Green op.127* (1997); *Joplinesque op.130* (1998)

Melody and Harmony for Guitarists
Andrés Segovia, As I Knew Him

for Sharon Isbin

JOAN BAEZ SUITE

I - FANTASIA

Fingering by Sharon Isbin

JOHN W. DUARTE
op.144 (2002)

Lively, lightly ♩ = 152-164

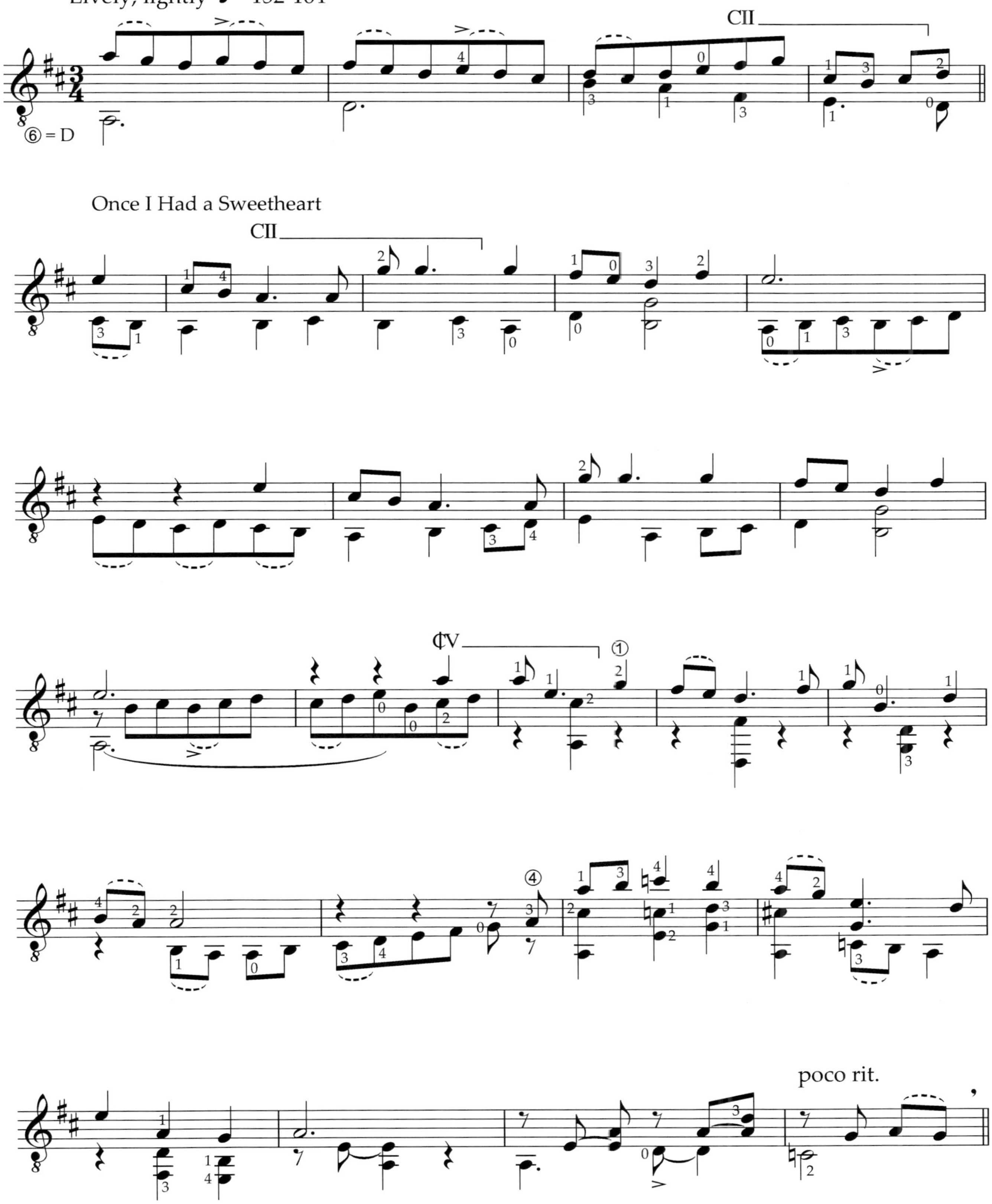

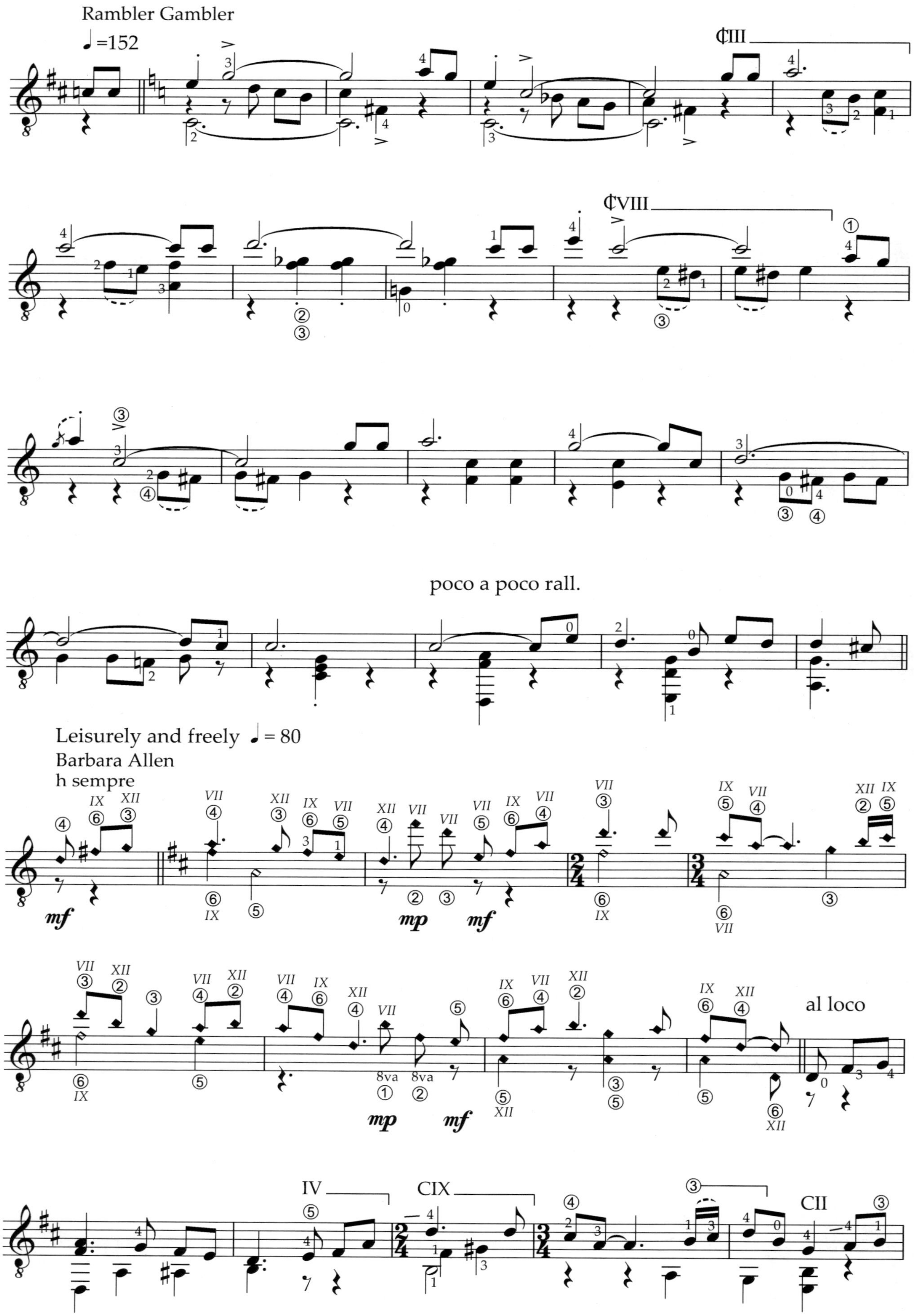
Rambler Gambler
♩=152
¢III
¢VIII
poco a poco rall.
Leisurely and freely ♩= 80
Barbara Allen
h sempre
mf
mp
mf
8va
8va
mp
mf
al loco
IV
CIX
CII

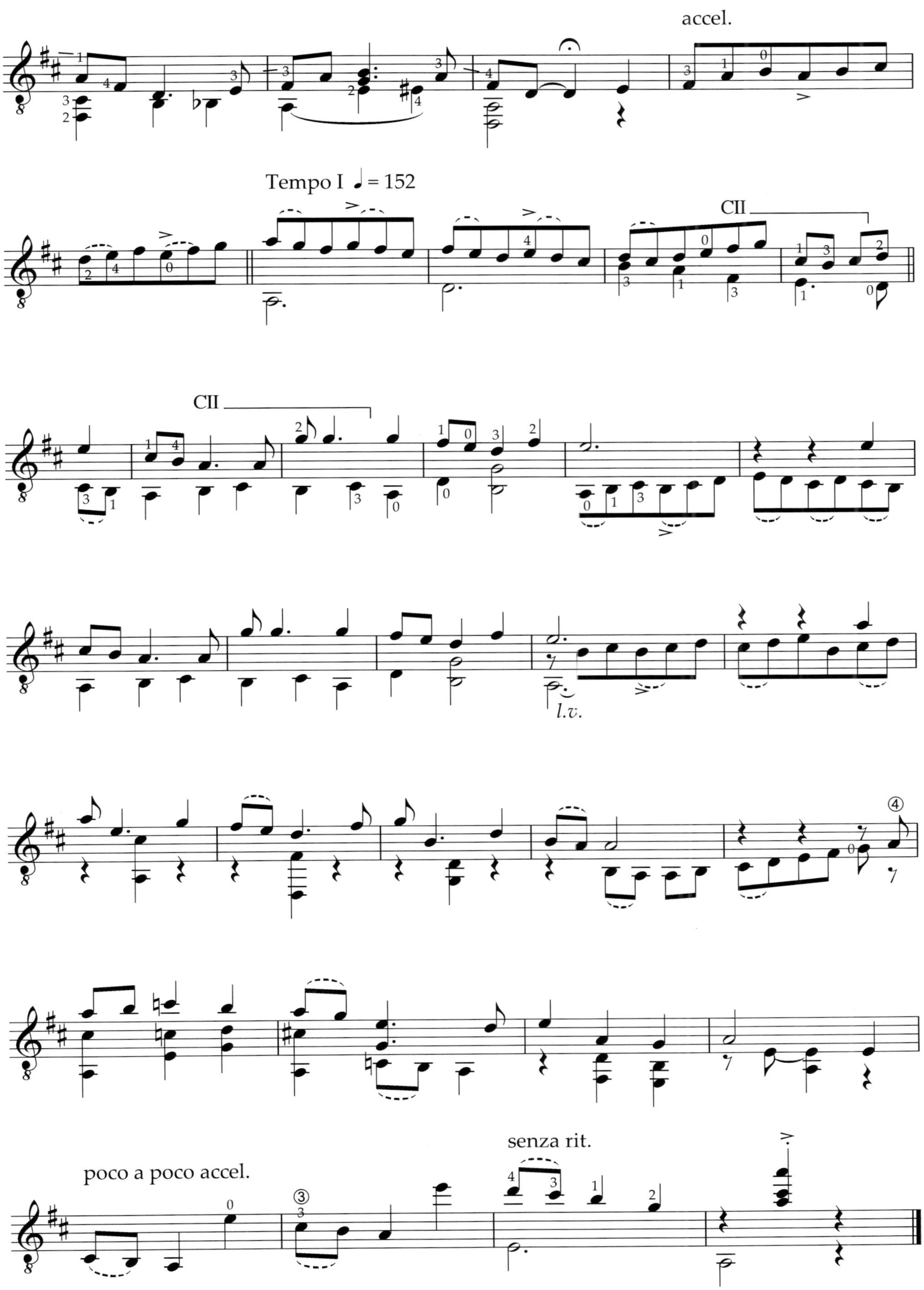
accel.
Tempo I ♩ = 152
CII
CII
l.v.
poco a poco accel.
senza rit.

II - HOUSE OF THE RISING SUN

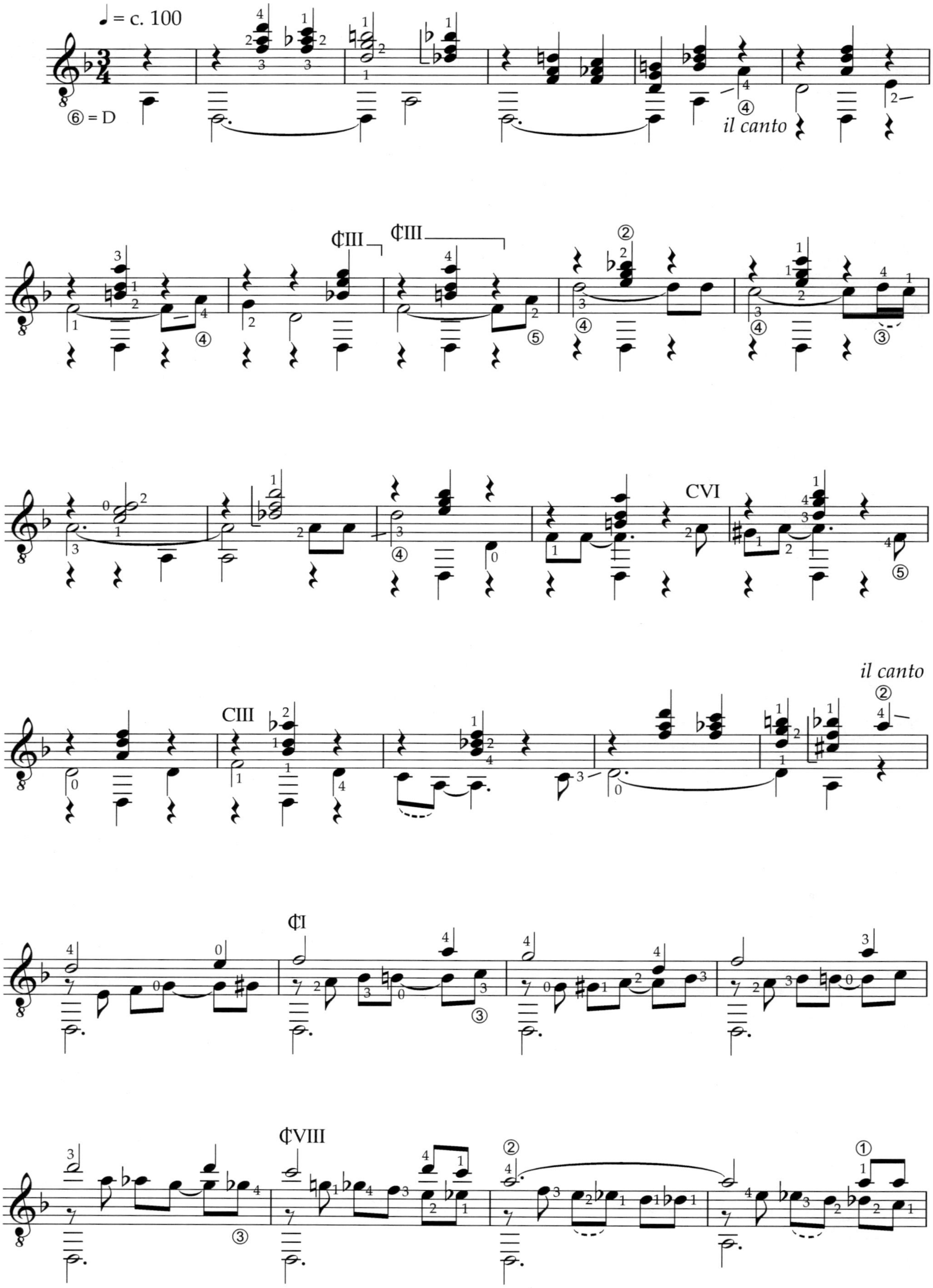

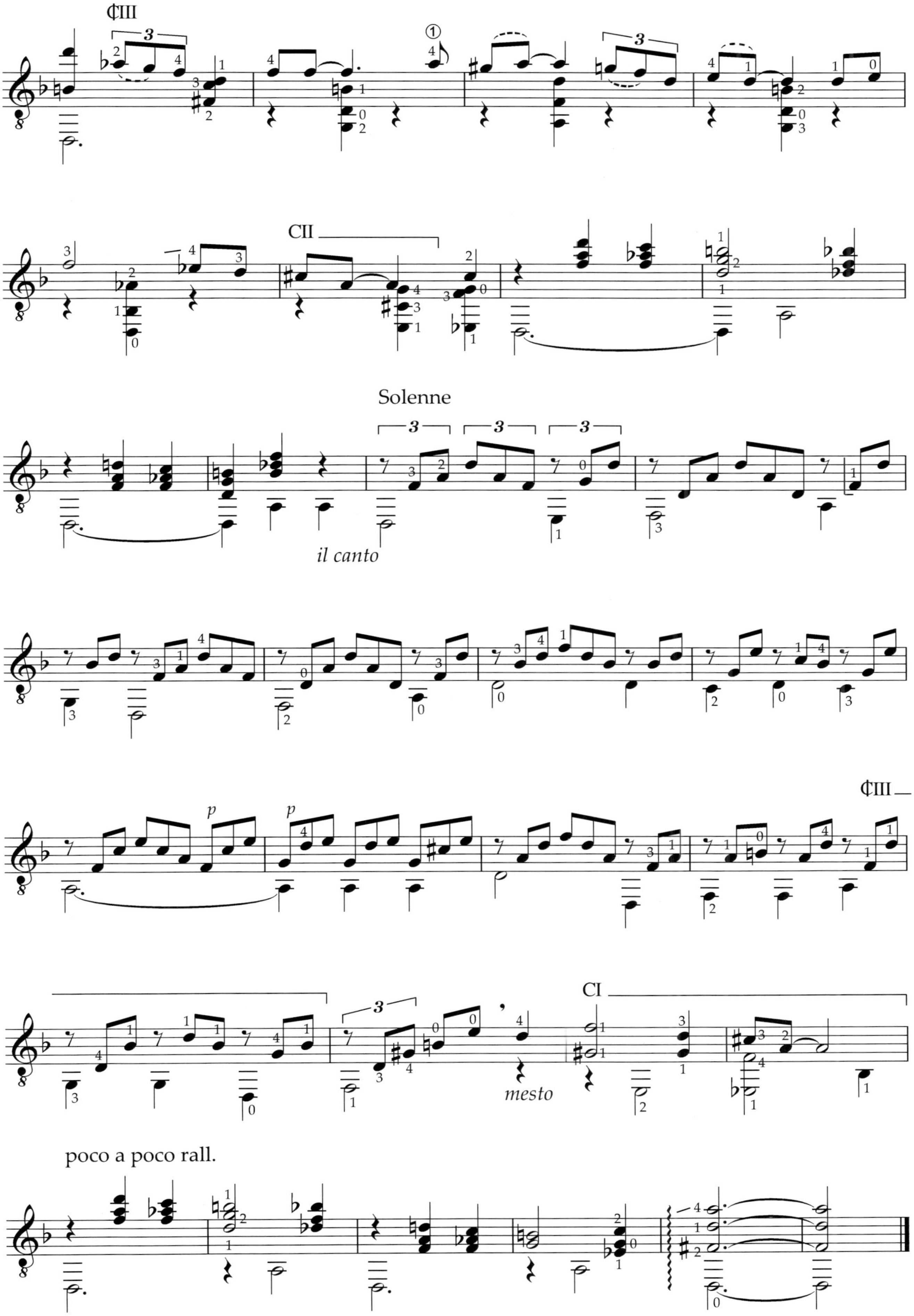
CIII
CII
Solenne
il canto
p
p
CIII
CI
mesto
poco a poco rall.

III - THE LILY OF THE WEST

Allegro ♩ = 152-156

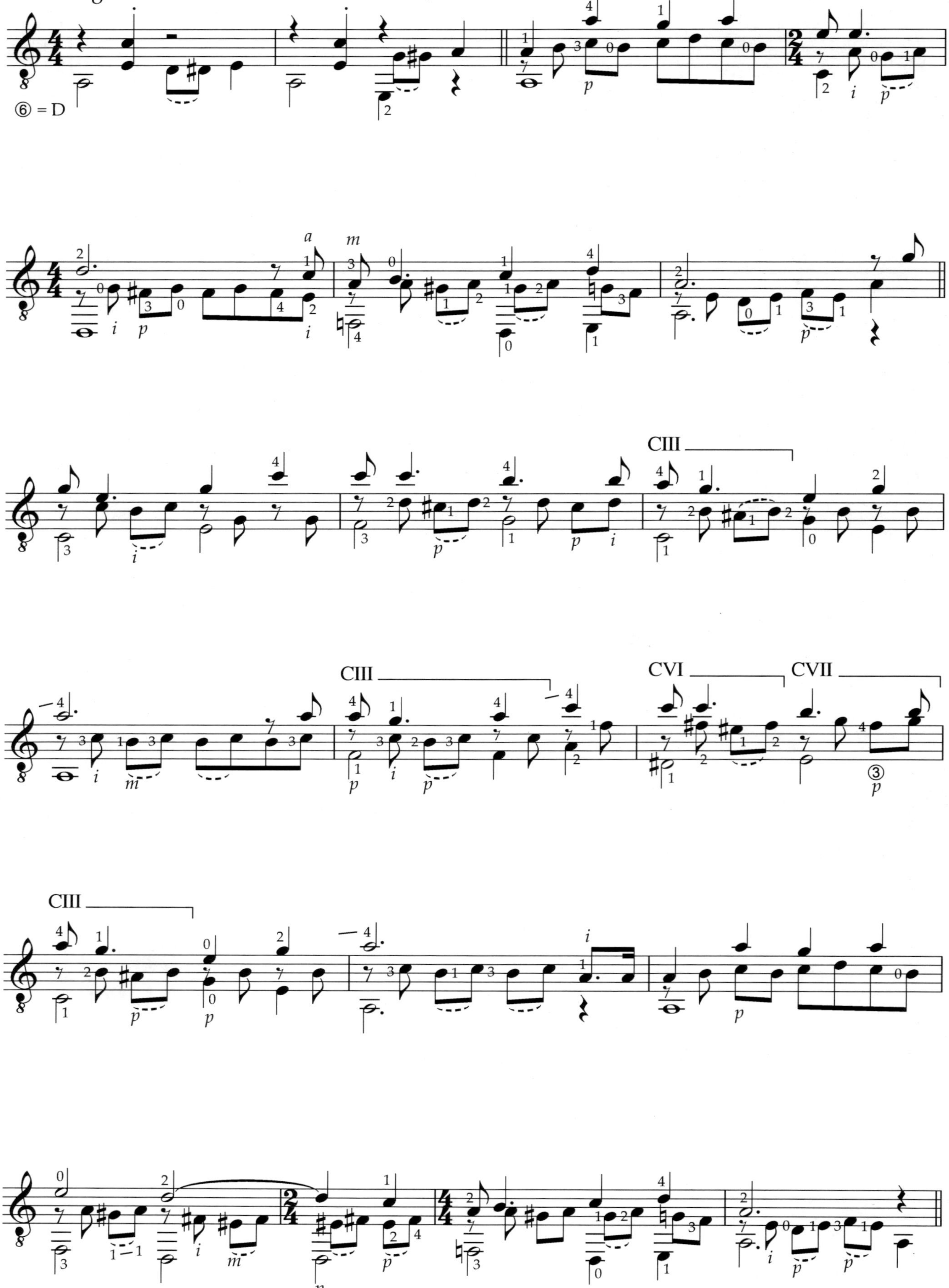

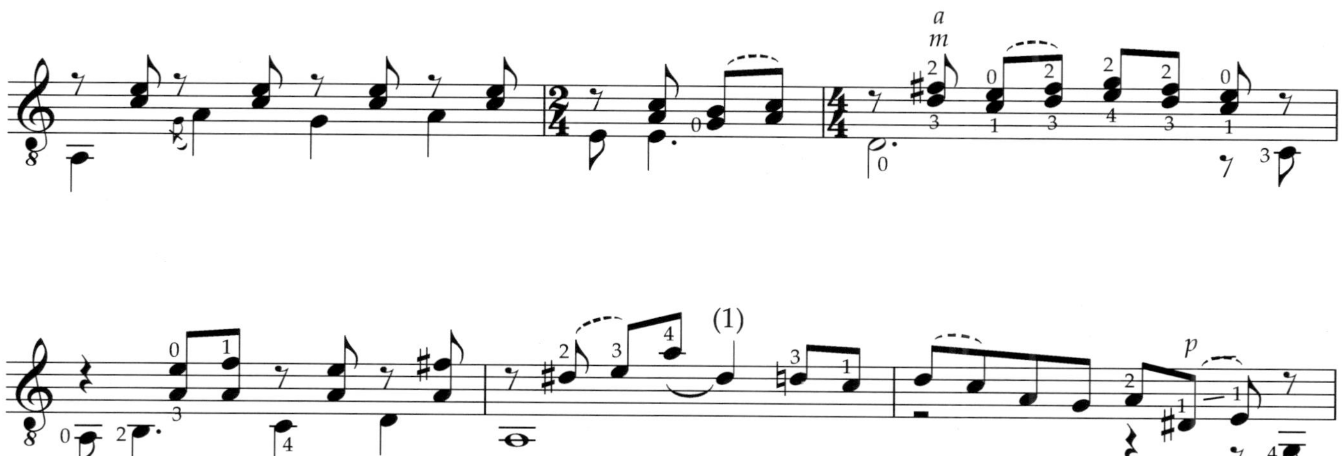

(1) Fret D natural, push string sideways

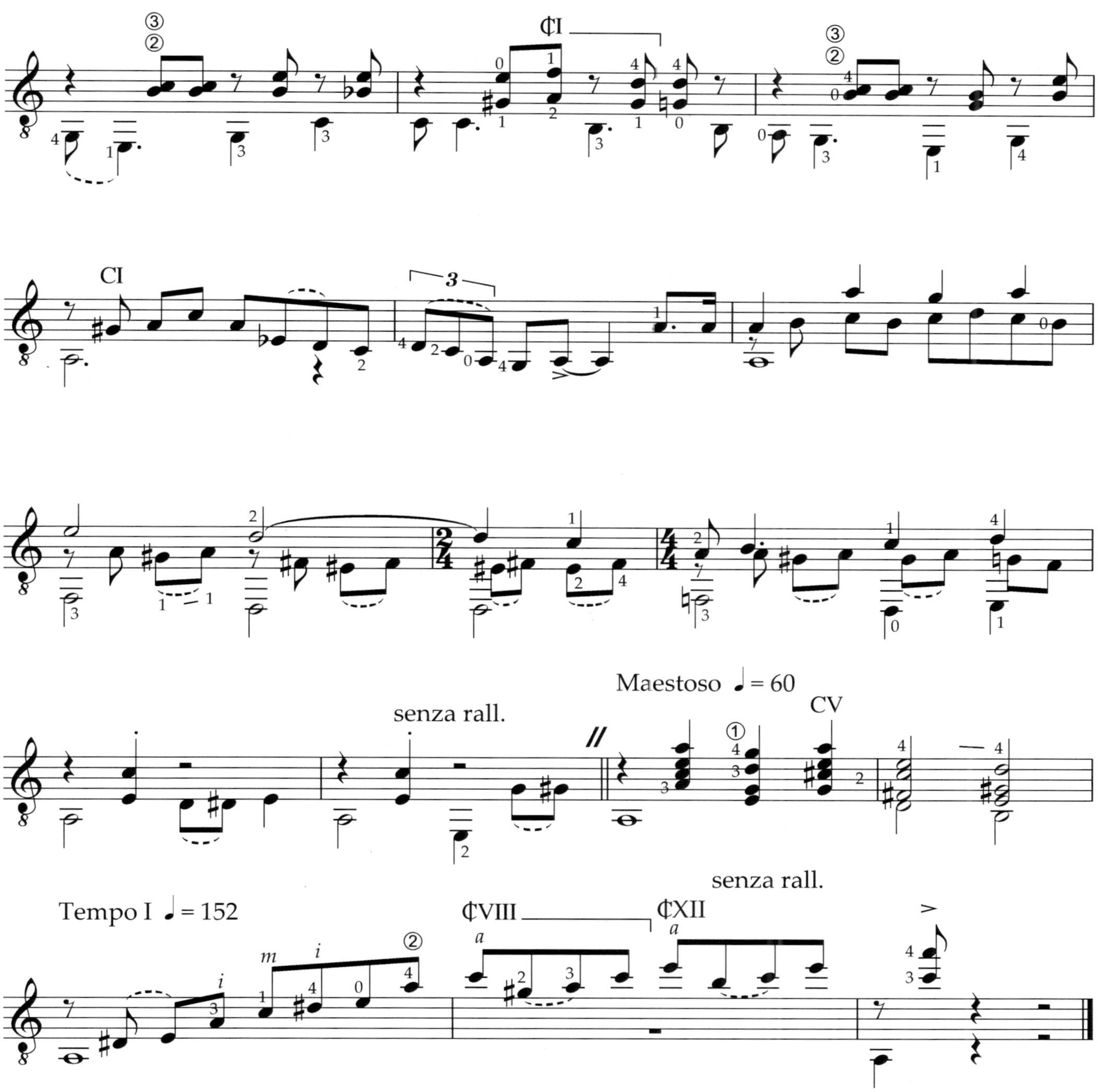

IV - THE UNQUIET GRAVE

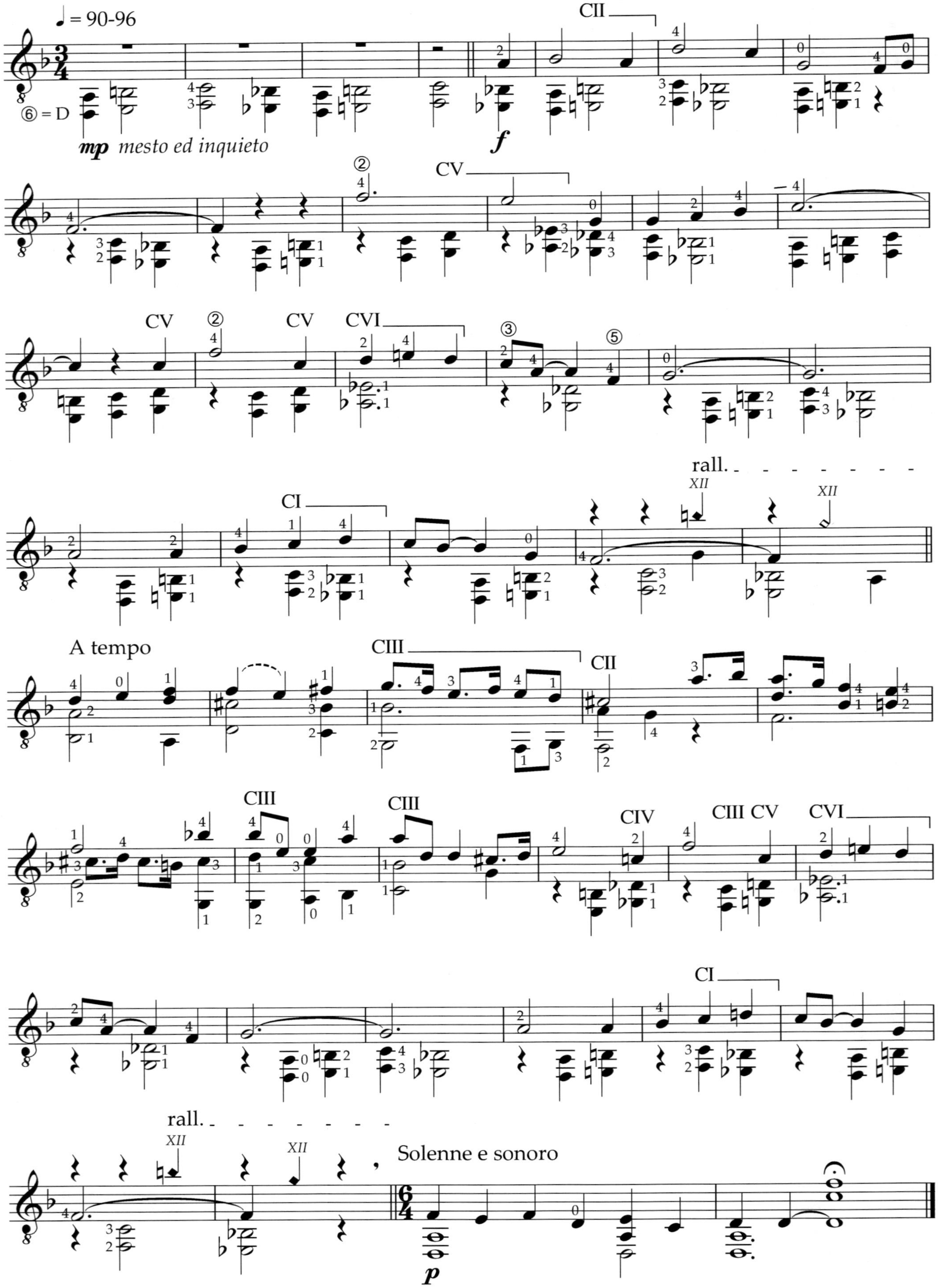

This page is left blank to avoid an awkward page turn.

V - SILKIE

Theme and Three Variations

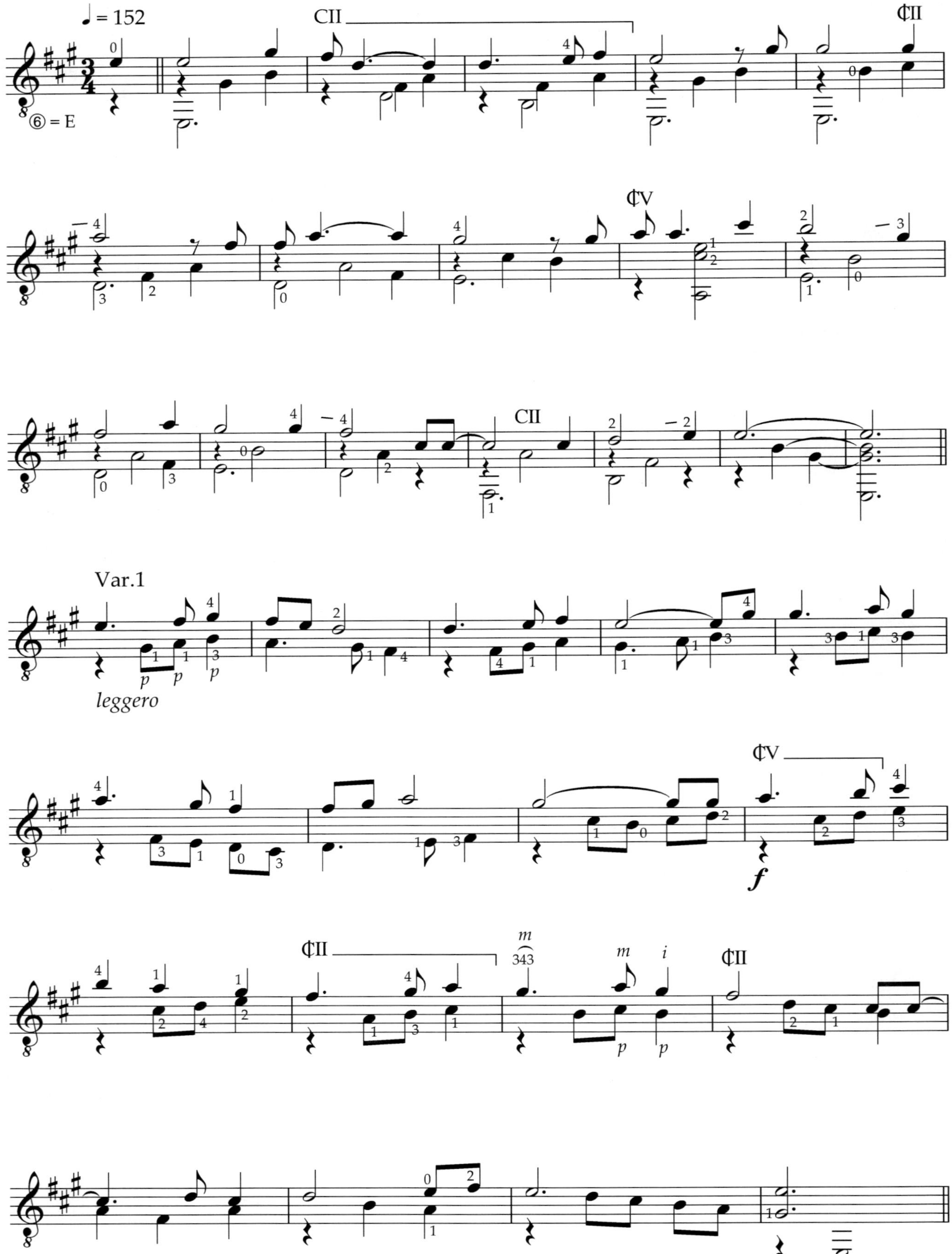

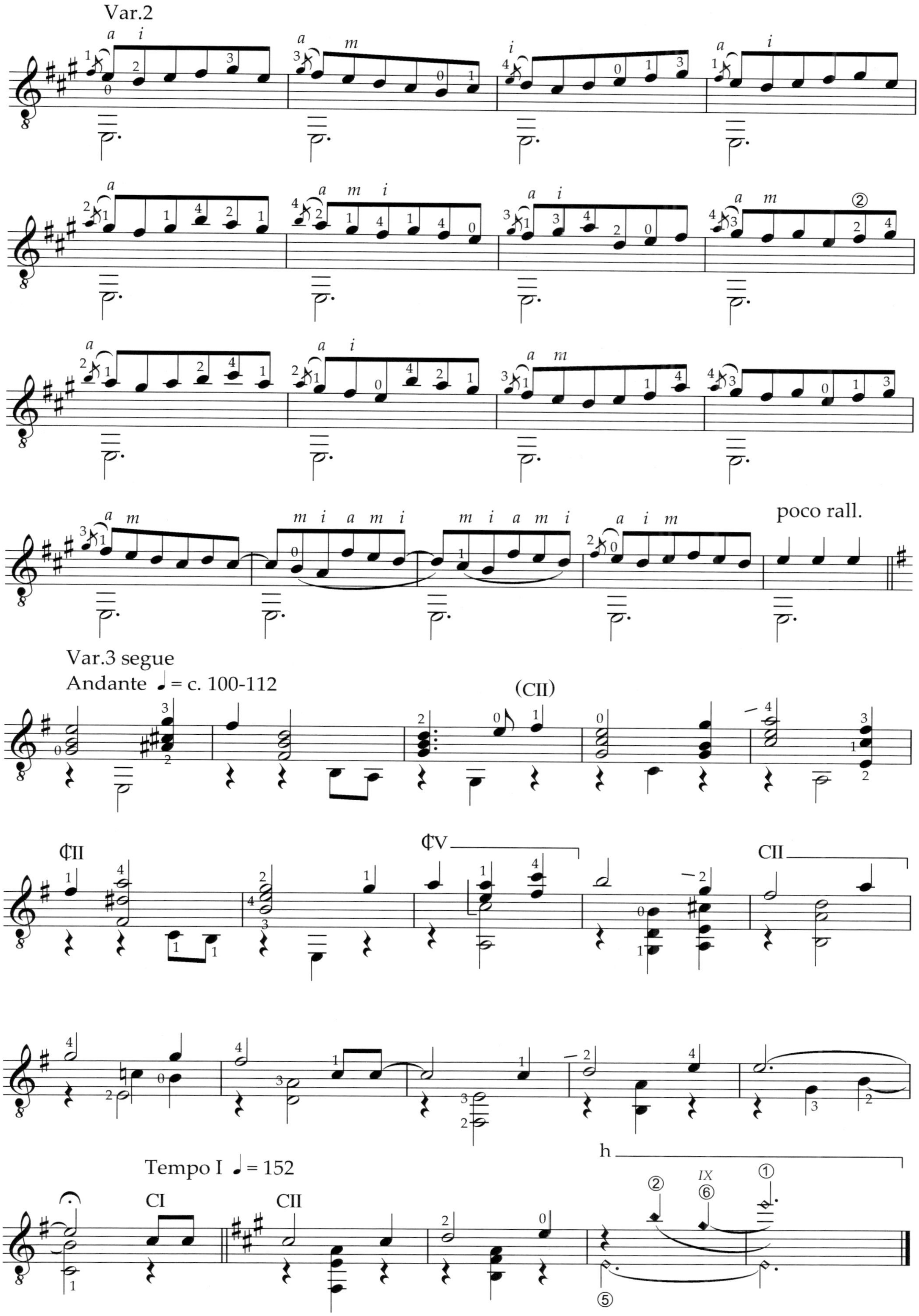
Var.2
poco rall.
Var.3 segue
Andante ♩= c. 100-112
(CII)
CII
CV
CII
Tempo I ♩= 152
CI
CII
h
IX

VI - Finale

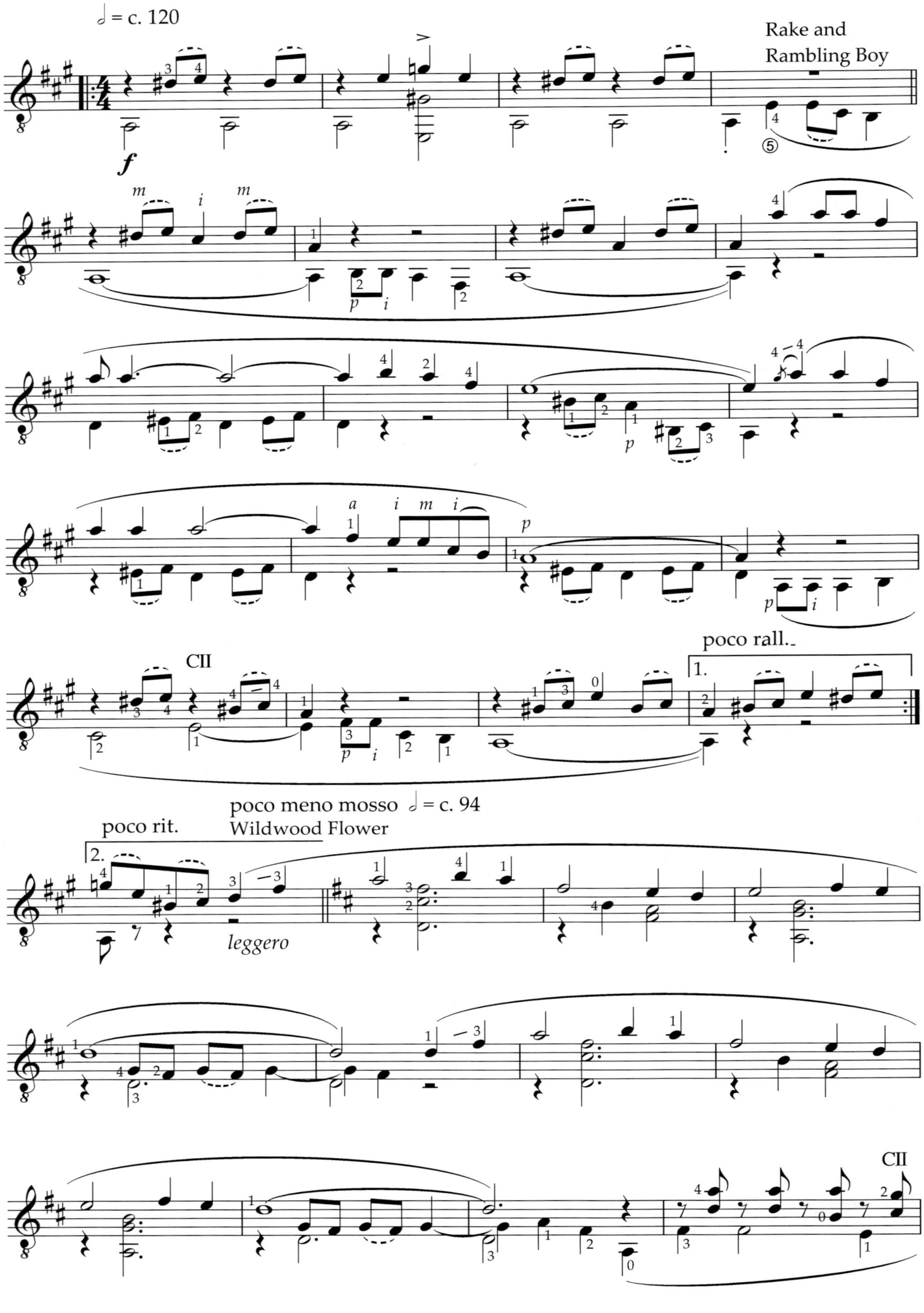

= c. 120
Rake and Rambling Boy
f
poco rall.
1.
CII
poco rit.
2.
poco meno mosso = c. 94
Wildwood Flower
leggero
p

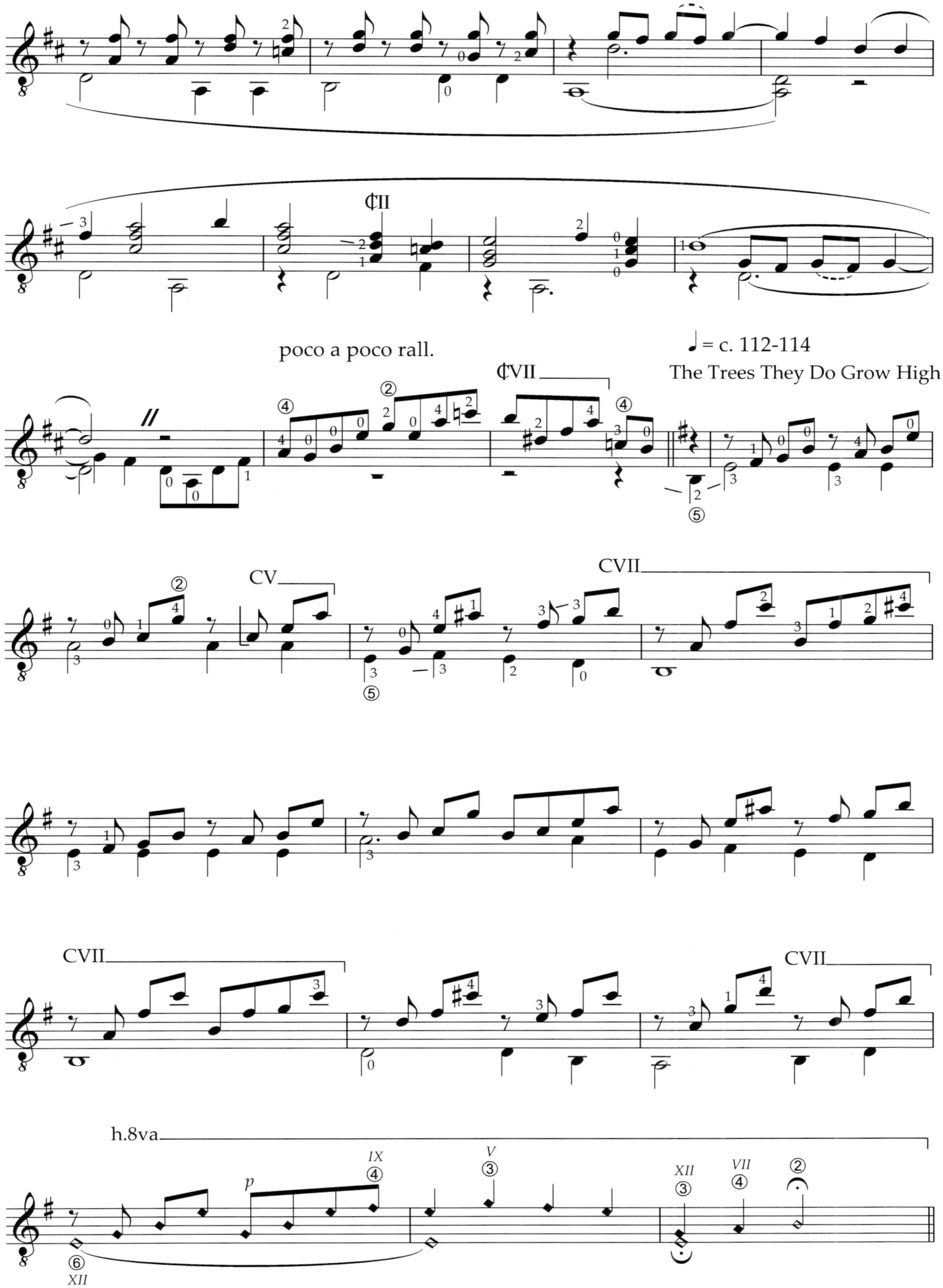
CII
poco a poco rall.
♩= c. 112-114
The Trees They Do Grow High
CVII
CV
CVII
CVII
CVII
h.8va
p

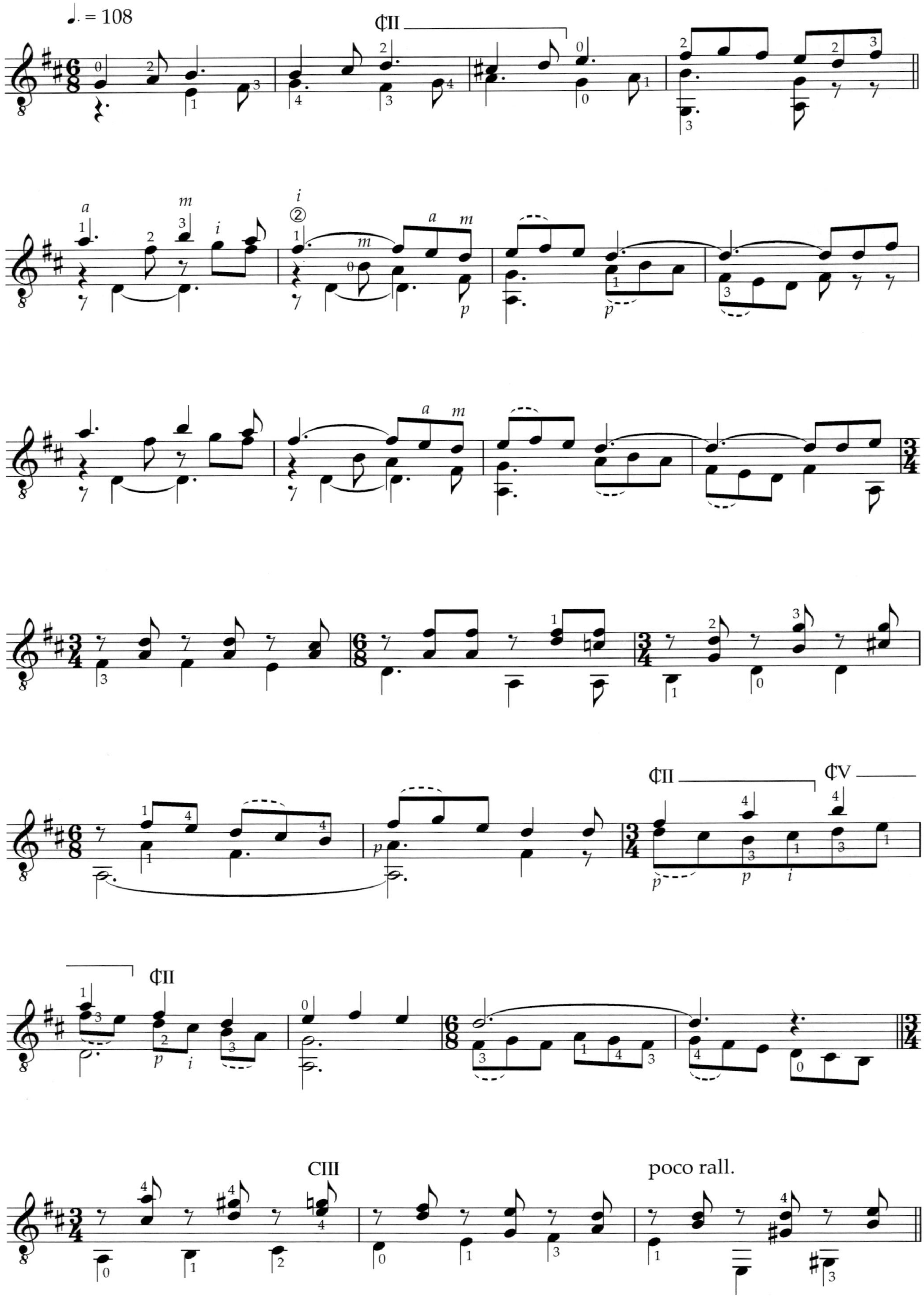
♩. = 108
CII
CV
CIII
poco rall.

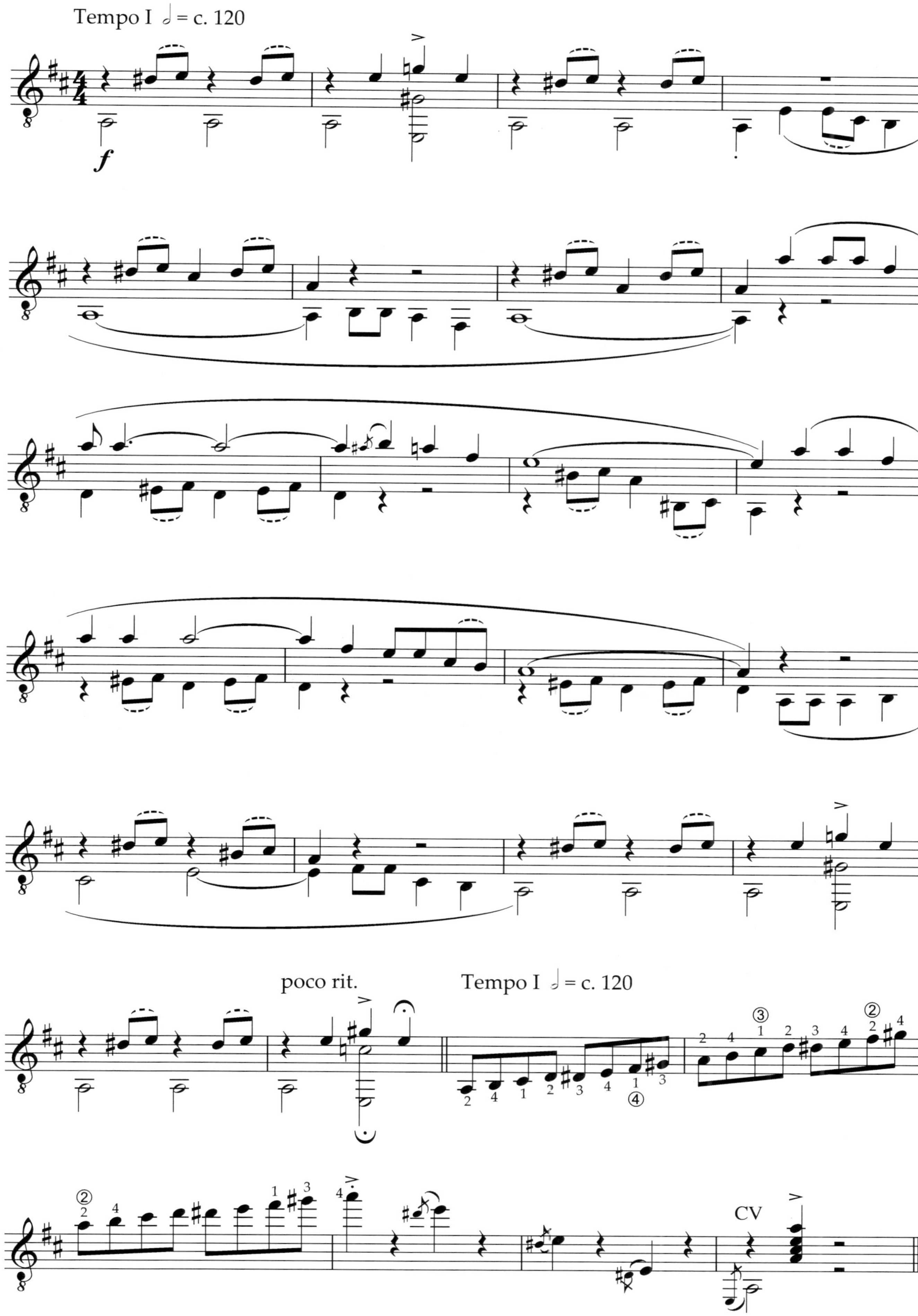
Tempo I 𝅗𝅥 = c. 120
poco rit.
Tempo I 𝅗𝅥 = c. 120
CV

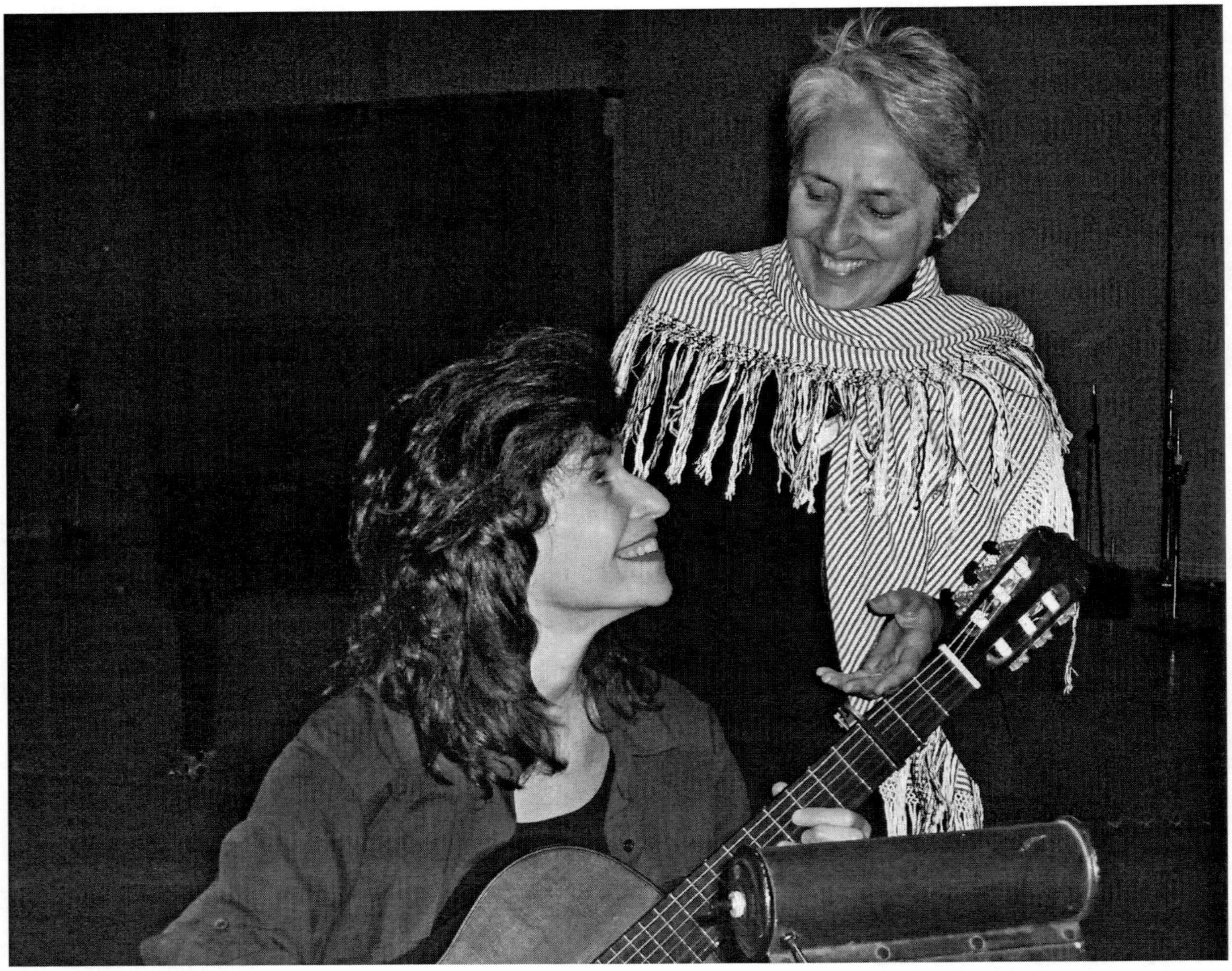

Sharon Isbin and Joan Baez recording in California - Photo courtesy of and © Sharon Isbin.